He Helps Me Rise

By
Rita Gottfred

DEDICATION

So many people have sown into my life through the years in so many ways and I am grateful.... Thanks to all of you all for your part in HISstory in my life.

Thank you most of all to my Lord, Jesus, who has never let me go, and continues to give me courage and help to be who He created me to be.... <u>His</u>!

Help us all, Lord to LIVE our lives. Reveal to us the desires of our hearts and allow them to bear fruit, for in that we will see the fulfillment of Your heart for us.

Table of Contents

Dedication	3
Welcome To The Dance	9
Chapter 1 - Introduction	11
Chapter 2 - The Song	13
Chapter 3 - The Story	19
Chapter 4 -- Recovering Your Balance	23
Chapter 5 – Things To Do Every Day	27
Chapter 6 - The Armor Of God	33
Chapter 7 - Wrap up of "The Must Do's"	37
Chapter 8 - Think On These Things	41
Rest	43
Love	45
Conversation	47
Encouragement	49
An Unselfish Attitude	51
Crisis	53
Being God With "Skin On"	55
The Father's Love	57
Don't Hold Back	59
Prayer	61
Move	63
His Strength	65
No Fear	67
Tenderness	69
What's YOUR Flavor?	71
Be Not Afraid	73
God Is Greater	75
Spiritual Warfare	77
Do Unto Others	79
Speak Up!	81
Correct Your Vision	83
Being Authentic	85
A Pure Heart	87
I Choose YOU!	89

Come!	91
Really?	93
New Life	95
Devotion	97
Rest (AGAIN)	99
Yield	101
It Is What It Is	103
At Your Wit's End	105
Why Pray?	107
Faith	109
Let's Talk About It	111
Daddy Catch Me	113
Whose Are You?	115
Allow Him to Write Your Day	117
The Aim	119
What WOULD Jesus Do?	121
Measures	123
Blend, But Don't Bend	125
Here... There... Or In The Air	127
Take Down The Wall	129
God's Purpose	131
What IS Sin?	133
Help for Past Traumas	135
Mission Accomplished	137
Help In Weakness	139
And Finally	141
Chapter 9 – The Reality of Retirement	143

"Do Every Day"	147-148

Designed to be cut out for your use.

All verses are quoted from the WEB
(World English Bible translation)
For purposes of public domain.

Feel free to check them out
in your favorite translation!

A few years ago my husband gave me this little picture holder in the shape of a high heeled shoe... I felt I was to make a little sign to put on it's coil instead of a picture.... It was to just say

"Welcome To The Dance"

It was as if the Lord of the Dance was asking me to take HIS hand and dance the floor with Him. I have never changed it, cause I always need a dance, don't you? I ask the Lord to dance YOU around the floor as you read my account of His healing touch.

Chapter 1
The Introduction

We all go through difficult things that consume our hearts and minds and leave us spent and asking questions.

>Am I enough?

>Is my marriage enough?

>Did I do enough?

>Have I loved enough?

>I can't hear you God... Do you still love me?

>Will you heal me?

I accepted that Jesus is my Savior when I was 8 years old. Young, you say? Yes, but it was very real and I became a worshiper very early. Music has always been important to me. It has been an expression of whatever was going on in my life for as long as I can remember. I've noticed that the Lord has used that love of music to give me a way to work through every difficult time I have faced.

When I was young, it was piano music. I played all those old hymns and youth choruses. I even found OLD (older than me) sheet music & played and sang it - different songs for different moods.. I sang them with all my heart and being. The Lord touched me over and over again and healed my heart thru His words and those melodies. As a teenager, it became singing - alone and with others - listening for those unique harmonies and life messages that always came. The songs were proof to me that I was loved no matter what questions and doubts attacked my heart and mind. There was always beauty in them and I found HE had given me a part to sing.

Sometimes that song was just words I heard or maybe a tune coupled with words that became alive in my spirit.

Sometimes the song has come from my Bible....scripture that sprung to life for me as I read it -"Oh that's what I'm going through!" "That's how I feel!" "Wow! That's really true for me too!"

Sometimes the song has come from a pop tune on the radio that spoke a simple truth to me. My heart jumped to life when I heard "I Hope You Dance" by Lee Ann Womack, after my father passed away and I saw him dancing around heaven fully healed with two hands instead of just the one he'd had most of his life here. He loved music so.

Sometimes the song has come from a friend or teacher speaking the truth to me. My high school science teacher, Mr. Nicodemus, once told me "Rita, you're the most normal kid I know!" Now as I got older, I thought maybe that wasn't the best thing I could have been - "normal" - (translated "average" to me), but it was just exactly what a high school kid needed at that moment.

Sometimes the song has come as words from a foe.... making me face a truth I had not faced and letting the Lord separate the lie the enemy wanted to speak to me from the bit of truth that WAS real and needed HIS healing touch. (Note: Every GOOD lie is spoken with SOME truth.... otherwise we wouldn't begin to believe the lie!)

And sometimes the song has come to me in the form of words that brought tears to my eyes as I let the icicles melt from around my heart so that I could bring the Lord the right questions for the answers I needed.

Always the song has been important to me. And not just the music itself, but the WORDS. I've come to recognize them as God's words of life to me.

Chapter 2
The Song

Has that decision to be a Christian from an early age kept me safe from any harm? No. But it has always reminded me that I am loved.... In fact, I am not alone AND that HE (The Lord God.... The Father, His Son, Jesus and The Holy Spirit....) loves us all.

A few years ago, I found myself questioning my personal life on my way to work. I don't remember what that question was... Why am I alone in this?... Did I do the right thing?.... Why are my parents sick?... Why is my hair frizzy?... It could have been anything!... As I tried to listen for an answer, some new words came to me so strongly I started writing them down. I had never gotten a song of my own before, but within 15 minutes, I had all the words written down. It just seemed to flow from a peaceful place within my heart and spirit and again spoke life to the situation I found myself in.

In the following years these words got me through a lot of difficult times. I did make up a little tune to go with the words, but mainly the **words** came as a warm blanket on a cool night to wrap me up and bring peace to my emotions. I was able to rest with them in mind. They even became my prayer for other people as I heard their hurts and struggles.

I called the song "He Helps Me Rise".

The words are as follows:

He Helps Me Rise
(Received March 2008)

I am a lion without fight...
A warrior laying down my sword...
I need Your fight... I need Your fire...
I need Your life......
I'm so tired, so distraught...
I can't see Your road for me...
I need Your eyes... I need Your dream...
I need Your help...
Help me rise!

Be my heart. Be my hope.
Be the life within my bones.
Bring Your fierceness for the fight,
roots that hold...
Give me aim for my life.
Help me hold against the strife.
Bring Your heaven here and now
with all Your might...

My foe tries to hold me down,
To mark his prize, to wear me out.
Still, his minions fear Your face,
their hope is lost...
Like gnats before a hurricane...
They can't stand before Your Name...
Breath of Life... Hope of all...
Blow them away!

Be my heart. Be my hope.
Be the life within my bones.
Bring Your fierceness for the fight,
Roots that hold...
Give me aim for my life
Help me hold against the strife.
Bring Your heaven here and now
With all Your might...

No longer lion without fight...
My sword flies with all His might...
He is fierce and brave and bright,
My life and fire...
He's my strength when I am weak...
He's my love beyond belief...
War with me, Lord... Reveal Yourself...
I will rise...

He helps me rise!

© October 2009

I have since been worried about many real life issues....

My parents getting older and ill... fighting for their lives and needing our help... while my brother and I were still working full time... and then their deaths a little over a year apart.

Me as well as some of my family members losing jobs and not being able to find comparable ones...

Losing our home due to the downturn in the economy. Where will we live? How will we live?

Family and friend's worries - physical and emotional...

Losing friends...

Feeling alone...

Marriage woes...

FEELING my older age with my own body's new aches and pains and trying to decide what was problematic and what was just due to either not doing <u>enough</u> or too many activities and/or not "eating right"...

Not being able to lose weight and not knowing that older fatter person in the mirror.

Not being able to find things to do that I really had a passion for.... What does come next for me?

Depression....

When something felt overwhelming and about to swallow me up, I'd hear the song's words...

> **"My foe tries to hold me down.... Mark his prize and wear me out... still his minions fear Your face.... Their hope is gone! Like gnats before a hurricane... they can't stand against Your name. Breath of Life, Lord of all.... Blow them away!"**

And then I would hear that other voice.... the one I've come to know as the "enemy of my soul" who wants nothing less than failure for me.... He'd say...

>"That's way too simple a prayer..."

>"It's totally powerless...."

>"Some prayer warrior YOU are! Ha! Ha!"

"That's sort of like that "powerful prayer" you've been praying lately!" (That prayer was "Thank you, Father, that You're God and I don't have to be!"... A total reliance on Him...)

And I'd hear that True Voice and "the song's" words again....
(I called it the True Voice because it spoke encouragement and comfort to me as the Lord always does.) Truth!

"My foe tries to hold me down. Mark his prize and wear me down..." Still his minions fear YOUR face, their hope is lost.

This song I had been given, was MY song for the season, reminding me of God's overpowering awareness of whatever I was going through AND His love for me. It was a way to GET the ability to pray through the issues. These words have become an anthem for my life....

Chapter 3
The Story

As I said before, a few years ago I lost my father. I was a "Daddy's girl". He was my first and greatest hero, so the loss was great. A little over a year later my mother went home to be with the Lord also. We bumped heads at times, (probably because we were alike in so many ways) but I loved her dearly too.

They both loved to laugh... And STORIES!... They both told stories.... about growing up... about who I was.... about what was important to them.... about what would be important to me... about how to make plans...

They were not perfect people, but they loved me.... I always knew that. That's powerful – to know that even if you do it wrong, you are loved and respected - and I did not take that for granted. I've met many people in my life that have not had that blessing.

Even IF we have that kind of support, we struggle to fit in... As children.... As students.... As employed adults.... As young married people.... As parents.... As grandparents.... As retired folks....

This book was born in the aftermath of losing my parents. By that time I had chosen to be retired from my "daytime job" and now I felt a very real loss of love also.

At 63 years old, I truly felt like an orphan that had no home (although I was married and had been for 30 years AND lived near my only sibling and my extended family of nieces and nephews, aunt and cousins who are precious to me) and on top of that I wasn't sure where my income would be coming from. Not a very good plan for the "golden years".

I am blessed to live in Florida on a peninsula with the Gulf on one side and the bay on the other, so a trip to the water is 10-15 minutes away. The water became my place to go to be still and hear His (Father God's) voice of comfort. I'd go "to the bayou" (my special place at the water) to look out at the water and clouds as well as the fish, birds, and crabs at the water and planes that take off and land from the downtown airport. I'd get quiet to journal and "get in touch" with what was really going on in my heart and spirit. I WAS a lion without much fight and really couldn't see what, if anything, was next for me.

I remember asking the Lord what my purpose was now. I knew there were areas of my life I'd shoved under the carpet to deal with later because I was "busy" or "too tired", but by this time some of them seemed overwhelming. And I heard the words of the song from my **True Voice**....

> "**Be my heart, be my hope, be the life within my bones. Bring Your fierceness for the fight... roots that hold. Give me aim for my life... Help me hold against the strife**"....

and I knew I was not alone!

Day by day I went to the water and I went to the Lord.... I read books on weight control and exercise and took steps to love myself more... I listened to songs and worshipped aloud and quietly with my iPod, iPhone or the radio.... I cried out my despair and losses.... I prayed with words I understood and words I didn't.... and I wrote page after page of journals spilling my life - good, not so good, and ugly - before the Lord. Also in my journal, I wrote the words I thought He spoke back to me - the encouragements and peace I sensed Him saying.

Eventually I got a plan for survival and recovery. They were specific steps for me to follow every day... steps to wholeness once again. I want to share them with you. They are not written in stone. Some will be helpful to you and some will be just good thoughts and some you may totally disagree with. Whatever happens, my desire is only for you to use them as a springboard to what the Lord has for you.

I realize that God is ALWAYS teaching us. We never remain stagnant. As we understand more we see more. I don't think we ever arrive until He takes us home for eternity - and I'm not sure of that mansion in the sky and what all THAT entails, but I do know our earthly tears don't follow us there AND He provides all we need for that "life" as well!

Chapter 4
Recovering Your Balance

Recovery or Healing from whatever you've experienced is a **road** to be travelled... A process... It doesn't happen all at once.... When you've been knocked off balance, it's a steady letting go of what you don't need or have any longer and an acceptance of new thoughts or behaviors and facing what IS now. In my case I was letting go of "family" and "life" as I knew it and finding out what my next season of life was going to be.

No matter what you are recovering from, some of the feelings are the same...

Feelings of Fear...

Feeling Sadness...

Feeling "down" or downright depressed...

How do I now face the things I must?

Feeling guilty - "Why didn't I take care of this?"...

And MAYBE there's some **anger** thrown in there too!!!

Why are they doing that?

I'm a Christian and you're supposed to take care of me, God!

How can I feel this way?

What am I going to do NOW!?

This is not FAIR!

I had taught myself to ignore many of these feelings and just do what I thought needed to be done at the moment, so I needed to take time to even define what it was I WAS feeling.

I don't believe I thought up these "Recovery Steps" on my own. I did start my life's career path writing behavioral programs while working for The Department of Mental Health in Illinois many years ago, so some of them are just *planned* common sense, but some came to my heart and mind at just the right time for a particular situation. I've come to believe that's not happenstance, that's the LORD. And I believe these words are not just for me.... I've chosen to put them down on paper because they helped me and I believe they might just help you too as you're reading along....

I made several copies of the sections I was to "Do Every Day" and prayers that were helpful. I always had one near me as a reminder if I was "stuck". Routine is important at the beginning stages of recovery to get you off of square one.

I copied them. (I made more copies than I needed and stashed them in my purse... in my books... in my Bible... in my nightstand... by my favorite chair...)

I typed them into my computer so I could print them out in any size or shape I needed. (and I found it was helpful going over them by using another sense, touch, to go with sight and reading.)

I used a small 3x4 address notebook and put the plan in it and kept it in my purse.

I made a 5x7 copy and put it in a small notebook beside my bed and living room chair.

I made another one that I put in my planning calendar – I also wrote in that what exercise (no matter how limited) I had done that day. I had an app on my phone that I could record what I had eaten for the day also. I made it all part of the plan and each time I looked at it, it sunk in just a little more.

(I put a copy of those pages at the back of this book so you could cut them out to get you started!)

I didn't use all of them every day, but I tried to make them available to remind me of what I needed to do. Remember...your healing is not dependent on a set of rules you must follow. Within these pages is a plan that will help you get to the questions you need to in order to ask for the Lord's help for the real issues. Be real with yourself and Him as to what you're really feeling and what is REALLY going on. We're not looking for drama here.... although the Lord's answers are often dramatic!

Do whatever you NEED to do to make a record of what you're doing. It will help you be accountable to yourself. You WILL slip up and not get anything done some days... Just ask for the Lord's help and start the day from that point... or maybe wait for the next day. (I found some days I had worked enough and just needed REST, so I gradually learned to REST.)

THE NEXT 3 CHAPTERS...
Things To Do Every Day, Chapter 5
The Armor of God, Chapter 6
and
Wrap Up of the Must Do's, Chapter 7

ARE IMPORTANT TO LOOK AT EVERY DAY...
AT LEAST IN THE BEGINNING OF YOUR RECOVERY.

FYI:
I STILL USE THIS PLAN OR PARTS OF IT WHENEVER I FIND MYSELF DEALING WITH EMOTIONS OR ISSUES I CAN'T SEEM TO GET AT ANY OTHER WAY...

Chapter 5
Things To Do Every Day

(To be used in conjunction with chapters 6 & 7)

This chapter, **Things to Do Every Day**, means just that! Make them a priority - early in the day to get your day off to a better start... But FACE THEM DAILY!

GET OUT OF BED -

GET rest and then get up! You may not be able to do this on your own. A simple place to start is a **vocalized** "Help, Lord!" (Yes, HEAR yourself say it!)

WASH YOUR FACE, PUT ON YOUR MAKEUP (OR SHAVE) AND MAKE YOURSELF PRESENTABLE

Get dressed, but NO CLOTHES with SPOTS or WRINKLES! Doing that helps you get out of the "La-La's" and into life. **GO DO IT NOW IF YOU HAVEN'T!** (and change those clothes if you're already dressed and they have spots!) I know sometimes it doesn't FEEL worth it, but it is!! (I've found that making my bed and straightening my surroundings helps also... If the room's messy, it's just harder to get my mind quiet to think or pray or rest.)

GET QUIET - HEALING IS GOING TO TAKE THE TIME IT TAKES! DON'T RUSH YOURSELF.

You are worth the time. Every day you need to hear that small voice speak truth to you.... If you have people who depend on you... (kids for instance... or jobs... or family), there are usually people who **do** want to help you, but don't always know how... When you need help, ask for it. Start with those people who know you've been through something and have said "Let me know if there's anything I can do..."

Remember though, the only one who can really give you grace for moving forward is the Lord. Friends or a self-help course – though they may be helpful and give you good tools – cannot totally fill that hole.

I've written down some of the truths that I heard.... Sometimes daily.... Sometimes sporadically.... But always healing and confirming.... They are words you often can't hear and believe from those around you for one reason or another, but when you hear His (Father God's) **True Voice** speak "This too shall pass", somehow you are able to hear and believe it. Remember His words always are helpful.... They are NEVER accusing. They always lead you to life, not away from it.

"SPEND TIME WITH ME" – God

So much grief is running through your mind. You need to hear HIS voice (and I felt He was saying He needs to hear ours too!)

ADDRESS UNPROCESSED PAIN...

Is there any unprocessed pain or suffering holding you back from life today? It can show up as a thought or even one word that you know doesn't feel helpful or hopeful as it moves around your thoughts.... A word that seems to be standing between you and your path to recovery, creating a wall or block to that path.... I called them "words on my wall". I've also heard this referred to as stinkin' thinkin'. Whatever you call it, it must be dealt with. When I find myself here, I usually pray, "Is there any word on my wall today, Lord?"

Many times I've found a word jump into my mind as I prayed that and realized that it represented something I needed to get past.... an unprocessed pain that I needed to bring to light and settle (could be as simple as a judgment I've made against someone else... or a pain that I felt because someone has upset my world with a word or action). It seemed easiest to imagine those words, if not dealt with, as stacking on top of each other to wall me off from the things and people that would enrich my life and actually help me heal.

Identify those words or feelings individually and lay them at HIS feet right away. I've found if I don't, those words will get tangled up with other ones already there and "VOILA!" the wall is built! You'll have cut yourself off from people or ideas and that won't allow you to heal as you need to. **What matters is that you address unprocessed suffering. That's where the words and feelings come from.**

"BE NOT AFRAID...I've got this!" - God

And remember....

ADMITTING YOUR PAIN OR SUFFERING WILL NOT HEAL IT...

BEING EMBARRASSED DOESN'T HEAL ANYTHING ABOUT WHAT YOU DID OR WHAT HAPPENED THAT CREATED THAT EMBARRASSMENT...

Embarrassment MAY cause you to realize there's a problem. Ask God to help you change whatever it was that brought you to this place. Then ask Him for help to forgive yourself and help you receive healing. Anything less will only allow that embarrassment to stop you SHORT of being healed.

PLACING ALL THAT HAS HAPPENED TO YOU AND YOUR FEELINGS ABOUT IT IN HIS HANDS AND ASKING HIM TO HELP YOU SEE IT DIFFERENTLY – <u>THAT'S HEALING!!!</u>

Remember that every good lie has some (usually just a small scrap of) truth in or related to it. Without that shred of truth, the lie wouldn't have much hold over us. It is usually something you would rather not face for one reason or another and seems overwhelming at the time.

The Lord will separate the truth from your enemy's lie and give you a path to walk out of the bondage of that lie. His truth will calm your panic and restore your breathing to normal. The thing that seemed like an awful truth will diminish and fade away – losing it's hold on you!

FEEDING OR OVERFEEDING YOURSELF IS ASKING FOOD TO GIVE YOU WHAT IT CANNOT.

Eating the wrong foods OR too much food, tastes and feels good for the moment but then it often becomes a lump in the pit of your belly or unwanted pounds that are harder to get off than they were to put on.

Only God's LOVE can give you what you really need... Tired? Get REST... Hurt? Angry? Insecure? Etc.?... Give it to the Lord. Only HE can fill THOSE holes! Craving food (or anything else... fill in the blank) is just your emotions refusing to be ignored.

HIS LOVE INVADES ME TO LOVE MYSELF.

Whether I find myself doing well or slipping, what is important is to keep seeking out His love.

Chapter 6
The Armor Of God

GET USED TO DOING THIS DAILY WITH CHAPTER 5, but also remember WHENEVER you're feeling slighted or hurt or in danger (mind, body or spirit) – **STOP** – **DROP** – PUT ON THE FULL ARMOR OF GOD **RIGHT THERE** – because the enemy of your soul IS out to do you in! Discouragement, Depression and Fear are the enemy's hallmarks.

Until the armor is on, you're not ready to go thru the fight. **Don't worry**, it's not up to you to save your life – HE'S fighting for you.

Ephesians 6:10-18

¹⁰"Finally, be strong in the Lord, and in the strength of his might."

You don't need to be defensive (with people or the enemy) Defensiveness only causes hardness and more obstacles to life.

¹¹"Put on the whole armor of God, that you may be able to stand against the wiles of the devil."

The Amplified Bible explains that armor as that of a heavily-armed soldier - which **God** supplies. I like that picture!

Sometimes I need to actually FEEL the armor going on... I start by going through each piece one by one trying to see and feel them in my imagination. At times I even need to move my arms and legs. And SOMETIMES I just ask the Lord to help me put them on... "It's just too much for me today!"

Whatever you do, I do think it's important to be aware of each piece's specific protection.

¹²"For our wrestling is not against flesh and blood, but against the principalities, against the powers, against the world's rulers of the darkness of this age, and against the spiritual forces of wickedness in the heavenly places. ¹³Therefore put on the whole armor of God, that you may be able to withstand in the evil day, and, having done all, to stand."

I see the posture of "standing" as a watchful - NOT fearful or guarding stance - but a simple "surveying" pose. The attitude is AWARE, but not WARY. Remember the words from the song...

> "like gnats before a hurricane...
> They can't stand against HIS name"!

The picture I see is of a athlete standing still... posed before the playing field KNOWING he is able to complete the task and WIN... Having CONFIDENCE.

¹⁴"Stand therefore, having the utility belt of truth buckled around your waist, and having put on the breastplate of righteousness,"

Truth for you and others. REAL truth, not just surface truth..... Your heart and spirit are covered. You're NOT GUARDED, but aware that nothing can come to you but what Father God can handle – He loves you most and perfectly.

¹⁵"and having fitted your feet with the preparation of the Good News of peace;"

Get your shoes on! Be ready! He's GOING to move and you want to move WITH Him! **EXPECTANCY is the operative word.**

¹⁶ "above all, taking up the shield of faith, with which you will be able to quench all the fiery darts of the evil one."

The shield extinguishes the flaming arrows of the evil one. The arrows land on it and bounce off – unable to hurt you. I will still cry from time to time, but the tears I cry from this point on are to empty out the hurts. They are HOLY TEARS – no longer self pity or long time regret. When they are no longer self-preservation, they become healing – for me AND the nations. It's a rippling effect that just keeps moving out from you to others you know to others they know and on and on.

¹⁷ "And take the helmet of salvation, and the sword of the Spirit, which is the word of God;"

The helmet is protection for your thoughts - knowing Jesus has paid for your sins and being aware of what has sprung to life for YOU from God's words....You know that you know that you know and won't be dissuaded from that! It's written on your heart. ("*For this is the covenant that I will make with the house of Israel. After those days, says the Lord; I will put my laws into their mind, I will also write them on their heart. I will be their God, and they will be my people*". Hebrews 8:10)

¹⁸ "with all prayer and requests, praying at all times in the Spirit,"

Pray with all kinds of prayers – music or recorded programs from your iPod or phone – Radio – Books – Heavenly Tongues – Songs – EVEN Rest. (I sometimes pray a simple "Lord, help me rest in You" when I lay down)

and being watchful to this end in all perseverance and requests for all the saints:

With all this in mind, be alive (I believe the Lord's given me the word "Alive" in place of "Alert"). Remember – others may cross your path – you're looking for who HE puts in your path. You'll know the difference... If not, TAKE IT TO THE LORD. He'll confirm or deny your involvement. You're looking for HIS path and HE will give you what you need for that. If you don't remember this, you'll wonder why you'll feel like you're spinning your wheels and going nowhere. It MAY be you're with the wrong people and the interaction is wearing you out!

All this doesn't mean that knowing the Lord makes everything easy. I think He sometimes asks us to do hard things, but He also gives us what we need to do them.

It ALSO doesn't mean that if you've "done it wrong", He can no longer move on your behalf! He can and

He WILL!

Chapter 7
Wrap Up of The Must Do's

I found it helpful to keep a prayer journal - writing down all those things that popped into my mind during my quiet time with God. It helped me focus my thoughts. I used it as a place where I poured out my thoughts and feelings to God and allowed HIM to speak back to me. The journal was meant to be for His and my eyes ONLY. He illuminated things I needed to address with others, but this notebook was private. I often threw it away when the pain was healed and I no longer needed to remember those things that were in it.

START WHERE YOU ARE
And ask questions.... Is this YOU, Lord?... What DO I do today?... etc.

> **"Which of you fathers, if your son asks for bread, will give him a stone? Or if he asks for a fish, he won't give him a snake instead of a fish, will he?" Luke 11:11**

BUILD ON THE FAITH YOU HAVE....
If it isn't strong, again, ask HIM for help to believe.

DON'T BE EMBROILED WITH NEGATIVITY –
Negativity is invasive. It can suck you in. Even when you don't believe all the negative things spoken to you or that YOU speak, hearing them rattle around in your brain makes it again FEEL that you're not making progress. We all NEED to see progress. Sometimes the negative is just emotion and isn't the truth.

NOTE TO SELF – TODAY IS A NEW DAY!

It's mine to "write" anew. Face the responsibility of that new chapter you're writing. "Am I writing this day from a perspective of powerLESSness" (the effect of negative or unhelpful emotional or behavioral patterns - learned habits that we use "to deal") "or of powerFULLness" (the effect of being infused by God's love)? He WILL infuse you if you ask Him for help to lay down the burden and take it away.

TREAT OTHERS KINDLY

My parents taught me that being selfish was not a good thing. Sharing and being nice was a high priority for them. If you're being "nicey" nice though, (defined as "just acting" nice because you "should" OR you want to "be better than they're being" OR because you "want something in return"), it can be dangerous.

This has been difficult for me as an adult... Oh, not being "nice" (kind)... I knew the difference between "nice" and "nicey nice" as well as "If you don't have something good to say, don't say anything at all" early. While that's not bad, it's not the whole truth.

Sometimes being "nice" stands in the way of actually facing and taking care of a situation. (From here on out referred to as "blowing it out, not sucking it up" which was the first spiritually helpful thing I heard in my recovery.) I address this a few times.... see page 59 "Don't Hold Back" and page 69 "Tenderness"... (I guess that tells you what MY biggest challenge was - especially at that time!)

Being nice (even if it's not "nicey nice") can result in us judging (condemning) others as "flawed". The Lord taught me it is MY job to keep the garden of MY heart weeded while trusting Him for the best for me and NOT judge (condemn) anyone else... OK I can hear those comments already...

"But we MUST judge the actions of others!"

Judging the actions is very different than judging (condemning) them, which is what I'm talking about here...

"Do we have to take everything that others pile on us?...".

Hear a resounding "NO!" The Lord MAY remove you from your situation to protect you or give you courage to speak up!

SPEND TIME DOING THINGS THAT CONTRIBUTE GOODNESS AND LIGHT TO YOUR HOME AND LIFE.
I'm retired, so I found time to do crafts…. to make those minor repairs to photo albums or clothes or furniture…. And to read books – creative books of all kinds - to nourish my spirit and help me be interested and interesting... but the main thing is you must find time for your own nourishment or you won't have anything to give to others AND you'll be envious that others even HAVE time for themselves.

USE YOUR EVENING TO CONCLUDE YOUR DAY POSITIVELY.
Ask HIM to bring you to a place of peace when you get stuck watching whatever goes across the TV screen – or screen of your mind – and you feel yourself sinking lower and lower!

You MAY need to move, talk to someone, or just admit "This isn't working!" Take up your journal and check for a "word on your wall"!

"I DON'T INTEND FOR YOU TO JUST PETER OUT! " -
God to Rita, June 28, 2012

That's just not how He wants us to live our lives... The end is in sight (None of us are getting younger...), but it can be the end of fussing and fighting too – a healing. He really doesn't intend for us to "just peter out".

SO.... Repeat after me...

I PUT MY LIFE AND STRENGTH
IN YOUR HANDS, LORD...

Chapter 8
Think On These Things

> "Finally, brothers, whatever things are true, whatever things are honorable, whatever things are just, whatever things are pure, whatever things are lovely, whatever things are of good report; if there is any virtue, and if there is any praise, think about these things" ...
>
> **Philippians 4:8**

During my quiet times, I listened for these "things"... and these following pages are some of the things I heard... I've separated them out, because they are random thoughts - not to be read quickly or necessarily in order, but they are and were **"True Voice"** (God) things that challenged me or spoke life to my spirit.

I've put them here as a springboard for you as you hear for yourself the many things He will speak to your heart.

But above all, remember....

> "Be Not Afraid..... I've got this! "
>
> (God... May 2012)

Rest

IF YOU NEED TO REST... REST!

I kept hearing that during recovery! It seems to be that we get so busy "trying to recover" that we forget to REST!

[28]"Come to me, all you who labor and are heavily burdened, and I will give you rest. [29]Take my yoke upon you, and learn from me, for I am gentle and humble in heart; and you will find rest for your souls. [30]For my yoke is easy, and my burden is light."

Matthew 11:28-30

LOVE LOOKS DIFFERENT
AT DIFFERENT TIMES

Sometimes the loving thing to do is to confront someone with regard to something - perhaps a difference or action that stands between you. Being loving is not always feeling warm and tender. Even when it's confrontation though, if it's LOVE (and not a feeling that manipulates... or a need to boost yourself up... or a need to cut someone else down because "I'm hurting" or "Well, they've hurt me!"...) I must surrender my resentments to Father God and ask for help in not picking them up again. That's the only way I will be truly free to give and get real LOVE.

Conversation

Listen and RESPOND

Listen - really listen - so you <u>can</u> respond or you may find yourself merely reacting with feelings. While feelings NEED to be felt and dealt with, they should not be allowed to rule. They change quickly and are not always reliable.

Reactions are like involuntary knee jerks because a nerve has been touched. It may not be helpful at all to a real discussion with God OR anyone else.

Lord, I give YOU my brain to re-work... Help me to truly listen and respond so I can grow together with those I love.

Encouragement

ENCOURAGE AND AFFIRM ONE ANOTHER

If you're living with someone else or just meeting people on the street or in the stores or workplace, be real, but be kind. EVERYONE - Even those who appear to be "together" - are going through their own "stuff"...

We ALL need true encouragement and affirmation. Find something you really appreciate in another person and tell them..

Their cooking...
Their kindness...
Their smile...
Their thoughts...
Their hair...
Their dress...
Anything to show you noticed them!

Doing this CAN be encouragement for you too!

HAVE AN UNSELFISH ATTITUDE

THIS DOESN'T MEAN THAT YOU'RE NOT IMPORTANT, but you're just recognizing that yours isn't the only "show" in town. (When we are hurting, it's easy to forget that - especially in our actions toward others.)

DEAL POSITIVELY WITH CRISIS SITUATIONS

There are things that only God the Father by His Holy Spirit can change in each of us. Ask him for help!

In a crisis, I've found it's always best for me not to <u>add</u> to the drama just to be heard. When I do, it usually adds to what must be dealt with for me to walk freely in a healthy relationship.

Being God With "Skin On"

BE GOD WITH "SKIN ON"
FOR WHOEVER GOD PUTS IN YOUR PATH

This term God with "skin on" is taken from a story I heard of a child who had a bad dream... His parent comforts him with... "It's OK." "Go back to sleep." "God will take care of you."... to which the child says, "I know, but I need God with skin on!"

People don't need you to be "nicey" nice, but TRULY nice. Listen to what their need is. We've learned to be nice at all costs, but people really **do** know when our niceness is not genuine... and that's not helpful to them at all. It's important for you to look for the people you can be genuine with.... often the very ones God has put on your path!

You are on this earth to be "God with skin on", so why not enjoy it instead of have to <u>work</u> at it?

THE FATHER'S LOVE

"YOU KNOW YOUR EARTHLY FATHER LOVED YOU... WE NEED TO MEET TOGETHER SO YOU'LL KNOW THAT I, YOUR HEAVENLY FATHER, LOVE YOU TOO."

If you don't know your earthly Father loved you, you STILL need to meet together with your Heavenly Father so He can pour his love all over you. He really does love us way beyond what any earthly person could.

Lord, let those who have never known a father's love, feel you holding them close – lovingly - in the palm of Your hand... safe from any harm - cherished!

Don't Hold Back

BLOW IT OUT, DON'T SUCK IT UP!

I have had a history of sinus infection flare-ups all my life. As an adult, they were fairly well under control, but when I would cry (which I can do over a good movie, an argument, a pretty picture, a grief or hurt or any number of things) I would try to just hold it in or sniff it back and attempt to get past it.

After my folks were both gone, trying to hold in the tears was setting off regular sinus headaches and infections. A dear friend told me to "Just let it out"... to cry and blow my nose until all the tears were gone... She didn't think that was a remarkable thing to say, but those words turned a light on for me! As I blew my nose every time I teared up, I noticed that there was nothing left to get infected.... It really was all gone!

This reminds me that other things I tend to hold onto and stuff down need to be blown out and dealt with to be healed.

PRAYER

LET YOUR PRAYER LANGUAGE CRACK OFF THE CRUSTINESS FROM YOUR EYES AND WAKE YOU TO SEE GOD'S LIGHT AND LIFE.

Your prayer language can include many things:
It can be a special prayer that you pray without thinking it through... in your own language or a heavenly one....

It can be a worship song that touches your heart....

It can be a song that speaks to you at the moment that isn't at all spiritual.

I've even found that sometimes praying my favorite scripture (or one that challenges me) gives me a springboard to have words to pray through to truth.... For example…. "Lord, I'm just not feeling this in my own head today, but You say it's right and true so help me make those changes that need to happen in my head and heart."

Sometimes praying and reading only the "red words" in the Bible is helpful because they are just what Jesus had to say and we consider him more trustworthy. Whatever it is at the moment... the prayer helps. Remember from the song....

"Like gnats before a hurricane.... They can't stand against Your name...."

MOVE

DON'T GET "CAUGHT" IN YOUR CHAIR. BE SURE YOU CAN MOVE FREELY....

Take a walk....

Get up and clean house....

Work in the yard.

Call a friend and invite them over for coffee....

There's a time to be quiet and a time to be involved...

HIS STRENGTH

²⁸"Haven't you known? Haven't you heard? The everlasting God, Yahweh, The Creator of the ends of the earth, doesn't faint. He isn't weary. His understanding is unsearchable. ²⁹He gives power to the weak. He increases the strength of him who has no might. ³⁰Even the youths faint and get weary, and the young men utterly fall; ³¹But those who wait for Yahweh will renew their strength. They will mount up with wings like eagles. They will run, and not be weary. They will walk, and not faint." Isaiah 40:28-31

As we trust Him, we notice – maybe little by little... maybe by bounding steps – some of that weakness just falls away.

NO FEAR

BE NOT AFRAID!

We hear a lot about "No Fear" these days. It's been used as a battle cry for all sorts of extreme actions that seem to cause people to "feel more alive". I don't think we need to be that extreme to face our fears OR to be alive.

Whatever you are afraid of, ask the Lord to deliver you from that. He wants us to live a confident life, not a fearful one. Sometimes it's not possible for you just <u>not</u> be afraid in and of yourself. You need to ask a trusted praying friend (I call those kind of friends my "prayer warriors") to help you pray through that fear. DO NOT ask someone who you observe is also afraid. They cannot help. You need someone who CAN believe. If you don't know anyone, ask the Lord to show you someone who has faith.

TENDERNESS

DON'T SUCK IT UP!

Here it is again... but worth repeating. "Sucking it up" by definition creates tension and hardness. As a teenager I was told by a youth leader in my church that I should not be ashamed of crying because that was "...just icicles melting from around my heart. It kept me tender." This thought really speaks to that word I got so long ago. Thank you, Mrs. Nicodemus!

Tenderness

DON'T SUCK IT UP

Here is a health myth worth regarding: Sadness. Now, my tradition dictates tears in add to deal... where I grew up was by a youth raised in my environment, it could not be assumed or cry on its own. Tears were there for the melting... from around my soul... me tenderness this thought evokes... speaks to that want of god to love again... that it stirs in me inside.

70

WHAT'S YOUR FLAVOR?

A LITTLE GINGER BRINGS OUT FLAVOR IN ALMOST ANY FRUIT!

What brings out your "flavor"? Usually, this is something others need from you that is of your nature and therefore requires no real effort on your part. Maybe we don't think it's a contribution, but others are enriched by the very presence of it.... Art, a beautiful use of words, or a song expression come to mind, but it could also be your ability to see what IS and call it out when no one else can.

BE NOT AFRAID

BE NOT AFRAID.... ASK THE LORD FOR A CHILDLIKE FAITH...

Trust Him... Then you can ask Him to take away your fear... Like the father talking to Jesus in this passage.

(Jesus speaking to the father of an epileptic)
[21]"He asked his father, How long has it been since this has come to him? He said, From childhood. [22]Often it has cast him both into the fire and into the water, to destroy him. But if you can do anything, have compassion on us, and help us. [23]Jesus said to him, If you can believe, all things are possible to him who believes. [24]Immediately the father of the child cried out with tears, I believe. Help my unbelief!"

Mark 9:21-24

GOD IS GREATER

WE DON'T WANT TO BE FEARFULLY FOCUSED ON SPIRITUAL WARFARE, BUT WE MUST ALSO REALIZE THAT SATAN WILL NOT IGNORE OUR PERSONAL WEAKNESS
(and we don't want to ignore **that** either!)

"You are of God, little children, and have overcome them; because greater is he who is in you than he who is in the world".   1 John 4:4

SPIRITUAL WARFARE

**SUBMIT YOURSELF TO GOD.
RESIST THE DEVIL AND HE WILL FLEE.**

"Be subject therefore to God. But resist the devil and he will flee from you."   James 4:7:
(if this seems impossible to do,
bring whatever it is to God)....

"Like gnats before a hurricane..."
From the song, *He Helps Me Rise*

DO UNTO OTHERS

¹⁸"The Spirit of the Lord is on me, because he has anointed me to preach good news to the poor.... He has sent me to heal the broken hearted, to proclaim release to the captives, recovering of sight to the blind, to deliver those who are crushed, ¹⁹and to proclaim the acceptable year of the Lord."

Luke 4:18-19

He's called us as His children to follow suit.
(Be God with "skin on")

You may have known this from an early age or maybe you are just awakening to the thought that you have anything to give...

SPEAK UP!

YOU DON'T HAVE TO MEASURE YOUR WORDS WITH OTHERS

This was actually in response to my unwillingness to speak honestly - especially to my husband, but sometimes others that I love as well - regarding things that bothered me. I tended to walk around those people "as on eggshells" not wanting to upset them, knowing they were dealing with stuff of their own. I learned that if I was speaking from a place of LOVE - to understand and be understood - I didn't need to do that.

PEOPLE ARE GOING TO DO WITH YOUR WORDS WHAT THEY WILL.... BE HONEST AND MAINTAIN YOUR CHILDLIKE FAITH, BUT GET OUT WHAT IS INSIDE.

This does NOT give us license to run roughshod over others! We need to be kind, but not indecisive. Stick to your beliefs.

Correct Your Vision

GIVE WHAT EVER IS TROUBLING YOU TO GOD AND ASK HIM TO HELP YOU SEE IT DIFFERENTLY.

Sometimes we just need to see something as God sees it... to get HIS perspective instead of our own blurry picture of it.

BEING AUTHENTIC

DON'T ALLOW YOURSELF FALSE COMPASSION OR ENLARGED PERSONAL EMOTION...

For example -

Perhaps you are indulging someone's behavior towards you because you don't want to confront them... or hurt them... or add to their stress...

OR

When you KNOW your feelings are perhaps a bit "overblown" (aka DRAMATIC) to get your point across...

Feel your hurts and blow them out... Face them and give them to Him... That makes room for HIS peace and love to flow in.

A Pure Heart

THE GRACE OF GOD FLOWS FROM A PURE HEART.

Keep it simple, just don't let <u>anything</u> keep you from His pure heart.

I Choose YOU!

"YOU HAVE NOT CHOSEN ME....
I HAVE CHOSEN YOU....!"

⁸"for by grace you have been saved through faith, and that not of yourselves; it is the gift of God, ⁹not of works, that no one would boast."
Ephesians 2:8-9

⁴⁴"No one can come to me unless the Father who sent me draws him, and I will raise him up in the last day."
John 6:44

COME!

COME UNTO ME!

Anything that makes you see yourself other than WITH HIM, separates you FROM Him – BE REAL! Through facing the truth with Him, you can allow the Father to show you what needs to change. You are not hopeless. Your situation is not hopeless. God is more than able to bring you through whatever it is to Himself.

[38]"For I am persuaded, that neither death, nor life, nor angels, nor principalities, nor things present, nor things to come, nor powers, [39]nor height, nor depth, nor any other created thing, will be able to separate us from the love of God, which is in Christ Jesus our Lord."

Romans 8:38-39

Really?

INTELLECTUALLY, MORALLY, SPIRITUALLY... BE REAL!

We sometimes hide behind a mask for protection. I felt by telling me to "Be Real", God was telling me I didn't need that mask anymore. He'd brought me to a place in my emotions that I knew He was with me and could change me AND my circumstances. It was time to open myself to what was real in all areas of my life and let Him touch them with HIS truth.

So... Whatever "it" is that you are dealing with, give it to the Lord and let HIM sort out what isn't His best for you and heal your need for it!

MY NEW LIFE MANIFESTS ITSELF IN CONSCIOUS REPENTANCE AND UNCONSCIOUS HOLINESS.

"New Life" here is referring to life after recovery. I don't think that we need to keep "repenting" for the life we lived before... Repentance in itself means that we turn away from the old and embrace the new. It is often the underlying cause that needs to get revealed... like peeling off an onion skin... We bring it to Him a layer at a time until we're at the core of the matter. Then He can take the need for THAT away and truly write HIS law on our hearts.

DEVOTION

DISCOURAGEMENT IS OFTEN DISENCHANTED SELF-LOVE...

I have an expectation of myself. When I don't MEET that expectation, I get discouraged. It raises the question for me "Is **that** who I really am.. or is **this**?" I begin to doubt myself and I shove feelings down to tame them so I don't have to deal with them. I MUST stay changeable and real in order to heal and grow.

AND THAT SELF-LOVE MAY BE <u>MY</u> PERCEPTION OF MY DEVOTION TO JESUS.

Ouch!....

I love Jesus, but if I hide in my perception of that devotion and don't let HIM speak to me of aspects in that love that may not be wholly healthy, I am limiting that love, that <u>devotion,</u> as well as how I experience HIS love for me.

When even our perceptions are taken away, what do we hold on to? Don't be afraid of the truth. Our God IS big enough to take care of what presently IS and bring us through to HIS truth for us.

Rest (Again)

ANYTHING THAT DISTURBS REST IN HIM MUST BE TAKEN CARE OF AT ONCE.... BRING IT TO JESUS....

and let HIM do your fighting.

"Cast your burden on Yahweh, and he will sustain you. He will never allow the righteous to be moved."
Psalms 55:22

YIELD

OUR LORD NEVER ASKS US TO "DECIDE" BUT TO "YIELD" TO HIM....

When I looked up those words, decide and yield, I found an interesting difference I had not noticed before... A synonym for "decide" was "call the shots" or "cast the dice". "Yield", however, has synonyms of "concede" or surrender"... things that would put HIM in the driver's seat... and then I understood...

It Is What It Is

CONTINUALLY BRING THE TRUTH INTO LIGHT. WORK IT OUT IN EVERY DOMAIN.

To NOT do that gives the enemy of your life a foothold. Once you have brought whatever it is that is NOT good but IS true to the Lord, it has begun to be dealt with. Only HE can change some things. The enemy will no longer have the ability to threaten you with it. The LORD will tell you the truth from HIS perspective and give you HIS peace that passes understanding... AND you will see progress!

AT YOUR WIT'S END

STOP, DROP AND

PRAY

WHEN A MAN IS AT HIS WIT'S END, IT IS NOT A COWARDLY THING TO PRAY.... IT'S THE <u>ONLY</u> THING TO DO... **PRAY**!

We need to see what is true in our lives and go to Him regarding them. Often the ONLY way to do that is to pray. Talk to Him as our best friend in the world... Which He IS!

WHY PRAY?

I THINK THE REAL POINT OF PRAYER IS THAT WE GET TO KNOW GOD HIMSELF.

The more we talk to Him... the more we know He listens to us - with ALL our weaknesses - the more we come to know HIM.

I remember in particular one time early in my marriage when I was thoroughly upset with my husband... I had tried to be a "Godly wife" and things were NOT getting better...! I finally said, "Lord, I must have really ticked you off if this is the BEST you have for me!" I heard silence for a short bit and then a small 'thought voice' said..."You're not exactly being all I gave Him either. I didn't give him someone who would only agree with him..." That was right! I'm usually a rather up front person who says what's on her mind... I had NOT been doing that for a while.

FAITH

FAITH IS UNDENIABLE TRUST IN GOD... TRUST WHICH NEVER DREAMS THAT HE WILL NOT STAND BY US.

I think of the song "Whom Shall I Fear" by Chris Tomlin. Love that song!

For a long time I'd find myself singing along to that song and hear myself say, He was "always **on** my side"... the Lord stopped me gently one day and said "No, I'm not always ON your side (thinking like me), but I'm ALWAYS **BY** your side...". There was such gentleness in His correction. Once again, I knew I was loved.

LET'S TALK ABOUT IT

TALK TO FATHER GOD ABOUT EVERYTHING AND EVERYTHING WILL BE STAMPED BY THE PRESENCE OF GOD.

This takes me back to a little book called "The Practice Of The Presence Of God", by Brother Lawrence. If you haven't read it, I recommend it.

Daddy Catch Me

HE CATCHES ME WHEN I JUMP.
AS HE LOVINGLY HOLDS ME, HE TELLS ME WHO I AM...

HIS!!!

Many of us have had the experience of saying "Daddy catch me!" to our earthly fathers. We needed assurance that he would and took delight that he did! Our heavenly father does too!

He loves you as no person could. You can be secure in His faithfulness to you. Only HE can give you the assurance that will fill your innermost need... knowing YOU are HIS!

WHOSE ARE YOU?

WHEN YOU ARE RIGHTLY RELATED TO GOD... WHEREVER YOU ARE... YOU ARE THERE <u>WITH</u> GOD.

Once you are able to trust that He died for YOUR sin, you are continually set free. His love touches you and you touch circumstances and others around you with His love. Its a ripple effect.

You WILL fulfill God's purpose as you stay in HIS light. (Remember... HE'S the one shining the light! If you don't see it, ask HIM. He'll show you.)

[5]"not that we are sufficient of ourselves, to account anything as from ourselves; but our sufficiency is from God;"
II Corinthians 3:5

ALLOW HIM TO WRITE YOUR DAY

I NEED A DAY OF PowerFULLness
(yielding to You)

NOT A DAY OF PowerLESSness
(surrounded by what I "can't" do.)

Help, Lord!

Come Holy Spirit... Do IN me what I cannot.

THE AIM

IF WE BELIEVE IN JESUS, IT IS NOT WHAT <u>WE</u> GAIN, BUT WHAT HE POURS THROUGH US THAT COUNTS.

WHAT WOULD JESUS DO?

COMMIT TO JESUS'S VIEW...

But realize it may be a different emphasis from what WE perceive as "What would Jesus do?"... Be sure to ask HIM, before heading out.

Jesus is GOD, We are not!

MEASURES

WE CANNOT MEASURE OUR LIFE BY WHAT WE PERCEIVE AS SUCCESS, BUT ONLY BY WHAT GOD POURS THROUGH US — AND <u>WE</u> CANNOT MEASURE <u>THAT</u> AT ALL.

BLEND, BUT DON'T BEND

THE ABILITY TO BLEND BUT NOT BEND IS UPON ME FOREVER!

Don't take on a wrong way of life, but enter the world and experience things from another point of view so you may have understanding and compassion. Then people may listen to YOU!

[22]"To the weak I became as weak, that I might gain the weak. I have become all things to all men, that I may by all means save some."
I Corinthians 9:22

Here... There... Or In The Air!

"FROM SUNRISE TO SUNSET (AND BEYOND TO REST), MY ACQUIRED SEASON HAS BEEN ESTABLISHED IN THE HEAVENLIES AND IS MANIFESTING IN THE EARTH REALM"

"My acquired season" refers to what is going on in my life NOW. One day as I was at the bayou, I wondered what was left for me in my life... I had often said goodbye to family and friends. Sometimes they were gone to me through death, but sometimes it was because one of us was moving. I didn't KNOW if or when I'd see them again on this side of heaven. It became a goodbye statement to say I'd see them "Here... There... Or In the Air (Heaven)!" It's good to truly believe that no matter what comes, God has gone before and will go behind me. I need not fear.

TAKE DOWN THE WALL

EVERYTHING WHICH ERECTS ITSELF AS A BARRIER AGAINST THE KNOWLEDGE OF GOD MUST BE DEMOLISHED BY DRAWING ON GOD'S POWER, <u>NOT</u> BY FLESHLY ENDEAVOR OR COMPROMISE.

To get thru ANYTHING that stands between you and God – even any <u>little</u> irritation – face it! Don't stuff it down or ignore it or the wall will soon be built. Bring the irritation or other barrier to the Lord, and He'll be glorified in the healing of it.

> **"for the weapons of our warfare are not of the flesh, but mighty before God to the throwing down of strongholds"**
> **II Corinthians 10:4**

Those "little things" are what that stronghold is comprised of!

God's Purpose

IF YOU CHOOSE TO AGREE WITH GOD'S PURPOSE, HE WILL BRING IT ABOUT, NOT ONLY IN THAT INSTANCE, BUT OTHER INSTANCES OF YOUR LIFE WHICH YOU CANNOT YET SEE.

Separate yourself from your own ambitions - or maybe even other's ambitions for you... Allow Him to move you when and where He wants and you will fulfill YOUR <u>true</u> desires. I believe He put those desires in your heart!

"Also delight yourself in Yahweh, and he will give you the desires of your heart."
                                                                Psalm 37:4

WHAT IS SIN?

SIN IS WRONG BEING – DELIBERATE AND EMPHATIC INDEPENDENCE OF GOD.

As you make your reliance totally on Him, He is able to deal with your sin.

Help For Past Traumas

Past traumas leave us with memories and emotions... Instead of life-giving effects of positive memories, painful memories can distort our emotions leaving a crippling effect on our lives – bondage to those deep wounds...

<u>BUT</u>, JESUS CAME TO RELEASE US FROM THOSE DISTORTIONS.

"The Lord Yahweh's Spirit is on me; because Yahweh has anointed me to preach good news to the humble. He has sent me to bind up the broken hearted, to proclaim liberty to the captives, and release to those who are bound;"

Isaiah 61:1

Mission Accomplished

THE GOD OF PEACE WILL SOON CRUSH SATAN UNDER YOUR FEET. THE GRACE OF OUR LORD JESUS BE WITH YOU.

".... His favor is for a lifetime. Weeping may stay for the night, but joy comes in the morning."
Psalm 30:5

Help In Weakness

THE SPIRIT HELPS US IN OUR WEAKNESS. HE INTERCEDES FOR US WITH GROANS THAT WORDS CANNOT EXPRESS...

"In the same way, the Spirit also helps our weaknesses, for we don't know how to pray as we ought. But the Spirit himself makes intercession for us with groanings which can't be uttered."

Romans 8:26

AND FINALLY

PRAY TO THE ONE WHO HAS ALREADY DEFEATED OUR ENEMY!!!

Ask Him to release the Army of Heaven to defend you!

Chapter 9
The REALITY of Retirement....

(I wrote this shortly after I retired...)

Ahh... boredom... It's a kicker alright. I like to get out and go. Sitting around just makes me feel "lazy". It IS a state of mind though, not reality. "I shouldn't be doing this...", "Surely there's **something** I should be doing..." etc, etc. And because I "FEEL" lazy I want food or some other comfort!

I'm trying to find what makes me come alive inside today. It's different from last year or 5 years ago. My job did a lot of that then. "Got to get this and that done." Now it's more a thing of "what are you going to do now?"

I don't know what you do for meditation, but "navel gazing" was always a dangerous place for me. It pulled up a lot of emotions that I usually kept stuffed down without getting relief from them. I have to go to something that's bigger than me.

It's become the Lord... Worshipping Him for who He is and what He's done in my life... Realizing where He's picked me up and set my feet on solid ground when I really couldn't stand by myself for one reason or another... Realizing that He loves me more than anyone has or ever could love me...

I'm not sure He has a definite plan for my life in that it is only one true ambition... I rather think it's more like Him saying to me "Kid I really love you and delight in you. You're something! What do you want to do today?" He's already written His law on my heart when I accepted Him as MY Redeemer... My path to Father God.

My favorite verse for most of my life has been **Isaiah 40:31**, KJV. Here I'm quoting from the World English Bible translation. **"But those who wait for Yahweh will renew their strength. They will mount up with wings like eagles. They will run, and not be weary. They will walk, and not faint."**

So..... I pray the Lord shows you how much HE loves you today. Shows you the wonderful gift He gave Himself of YOU. How He is DELIGHTED in you. I also pray He comforts that place within you that strives – thinking you must DO more or BE more. He doesn't make junk. You are unique. The world needs uniqueness! We need to be reminded of that all the time. It's not just that we needed it back when we were forming our opinions and business selves.... He is new every morning. If we could ever really harness that thought, we could be new every morning as well... and no longer bored!

"Love you girl (or guy)!
Hope you have a great day!"
-God

The End of my story
(But just the beginning....)

(This page is designed to be pulled out for your convenience - taken from Chapters 5, 6, & 7)

Things To Do Every Day
• Get up, wash at least your face, put on makeup (or shave) and make yourself presentable. (no clothes with spots on them) Gets you out of the La-La's and into life. GO DO IT NOW IF YOU HAVEN'T!
• Any words on your wall today? Identify them and lay them at HIS feet right away. If not they'll get tangled and VOILA! the wall is built! What matters is that you address unprocessed suffering.

Things To Remember
• Admitting the pain or suffering is NOT healing... Being embarrassed is NOT healing... Placing all that's happened AND my feelings about it in HIS hands and asking HIM to help me see it differently - THAT'S healing!
• Feeding or overfeeding yourself is asking food to give you what it CANNOT. Only God's LOVE can give you what you really need... Tired? Get REST... Hurt? Angry? Insecure? etc?... Give it to Jesus. Only HE can fill THOSE holes! Your craving food is just your emotions refusing to be ignored.
• HIS love invades me to love myself. Whether I find myself doing well or slipping, the key is I must keep searching out that love.
• Whenever you're feeling slighted or hurt or in danger - STOP - DROP - Put on the full armor of God right there - because the enemy of your soul IS out to do you in! Discouragement, Depression and Fear are HIS hallmarks. Until the armor is on, you're not ready to go thru the fight. Don't worry, it's not up to you to save your life - HE"S fighting for you. You won't need to be defensive (with people or the enemy). Defensiveness only causes more waves that must be crossed back over to continue life. "*Therefore put on the whole armor of God, that you may be able to withstand in the evil day, and, having done all, to stand." Ephesians 6:13.* (The posture of "standing" is watchful - NOT a fearful or guarding pose, but a simple "confident," "surveying" pose. The attitude is AWARE, but not WARY.)

  *Belt of Truth - truth for you and others. REAL truth, not surface truth.
  *Breastplate of Righteousness - Your heart and spirit are covered. You're NOT GUARDED, but aware that nothing can come to you but what Father God can handle - He loves you most and perfectly.
  *Feet Fitted with Readiness that comes from the Gospel of Peace. Ready to MOVE.
  *Shield of Faith - It extinguishes the flaming arrows of the evil one. The tears you cry from this point on are to empty out the hurts and are HOLY TEARS - no longer tears of self-pity or regret. When they are no longer self-preservation, they become healing - for you AND the nations.
  *Helmet of Salvation - you KNOW you are saved
  *Sword of the Spirit - which is the Word of God. **You KNOW that you know that you know!**

• And PRAY in the Spirit - all kinds of prayers - Words - Radio - Books - Tongues - Songs - iPhone - even Rest. With this in mind, be alive - Be "God With Skin On for whoever GOD puts in your path (not "nicey nice", but in all truth...) Remember - others may cross your path - you're looking for who HE puts in your path. You'll know the difference... If not, TAKE IT TO THE LORD. He'll confirm or deny and do your fighting.
• Build on strong faith - Don't be embroiled with negativity - Even though you don't REALLY believe all the negative things that are spoken, it FEELS again that you're not making progress. We ALL need to feel progress.
• Listen and RESPOND (not listen and react)
• Encourage and affirm one another
• Have an unselfish attitude - NOT that you're not important, just recognizing that yours isn't the only "show" in town.
• Deal positively with crisis situations.

- **Note to self** - is this day "written" from a perspective of powerLESSness (effect of habitual emotional or behavioral patters) or of powerFULLness (effect of being infused by God's love)?
- Spend time doing things that contribute goodness and light to your home and life. Remember LOVE looks different at different times, but even when it's confrontation, if it's LOVE (not manipulation and/or self-aggrandizement or to cut someone down because I'm hurting), I must surrender my resentments to Father God and ask for help in not picking them up again.
- **If you need to rest, REST** (That'll come up a lot. You're likely more tired than you think!)
- Use your evening to conclude your day positively (Ask HIM to bring you to a place of peace when you get stuck watching whatever goes across the TV or computer or phone screen and feel yourself sinking lower and lower!)

Words from your True Voice -

"BE NOT AFRAID...I've got this!" - God.

God doesn't intend for you to just "peter out"

Prayers flow freely from a place of childlike trust & faith

[26]...*the Spirit also helps our weaknesses, for we don't know how to pray as we ought. But the Spirit himself makes intercession for us with groanings which can't be uttered.* Romans 8:26

Pray to the One Who Has Already Defeated Our Enemy!!!
Ask Him to release the Army of Heaven to defend you.

The Lord Yahweh's Spirit is on me; because Yahweh has anointed me to preach good news to the humble. He has sent me to bind up the broken hearted, to proclaim liberty to the captives, and release to those who are bound; Isaiah 61:1

Help, Lord!
I put my life & strength in your hands

Words from The Song....

He Helps Me Rise

VERSE 1: I am a lion without fight... A warrior laying down my sword...
I need Your fight... I need Your fire... I need Your life.
I'm so tired, so distraught... I can't see Your road for me...
I need Your eyes... I need Your dream... I need Your help..
Help me rise!

CHORUS: Be my heart. Be my hope. Be the life within my bones.
Bring Your fierceness for the fight, roots that hold...
Give me aim for my life. Help me hold against the strife.
Bring Your heaven here and now with all Your might.

VERSE 2: My foe tries to hold me down, To mark his prize, to wear me out.
Still, his minions fear Your face, their hope is lost...
Like gnats before a hurricane... They can't stand before Your Name...
Breath of Life... Hope of all... Blow them away! (CHORUS)

VERSE 3: No longer lion without fight... My sword flies with all His might...
He is fierce and brave and bright, My life and fire...
He's my strength when I am weak... He's my love beyond belief...
War with me, Lord... Reveal Yourself... I will rise...
He helps me rise!

© October, 2009

All scriptures quoted from
the World English Bible (WEB)
in the Public Domain

Copyright © 2015 Rita Gottfred
All rights reserved for song and book.
ISBN:978-0-9896079-1-9

www.ingramcontent.com/pod-product-compliance
Lightning Source LLC
Chambersburg PA
CBHW061658040426
42446CB00010B/1802